Pinch Express of
Delicious Food

Angella M Ramos

This book is about food as a travel industry item and an encounter. It investigates its inclination, improvement, the board, promoting and dissemination

as well as food travelers - their inspirations and necessities, uses of data, assumptions and exercises. Of the bunch the travel industry items and encounters in the contemporary the travel industry scape, food is seemingly exceptional. It can

be a fascination by its own doing - an essential inspiration for an excursion, for example,

a visit through a wine district, an optional movement like lunch at a nearby bar

while visiting neighborhood sights, or a fundamental yet sub-par need as part

of another travel industry experience, for example, a

crate lunch served on a mentor visit.

It can likewise be a keepsake of an outing - a particular food item or refreshment

brought back to impart to loved ones. The taste or smell from a

food item can invoke recollections and the longing to get back to the spot

represented by the taste or smell. For sure, food is both a representative encounter as well as an actual item. It is in many cases co-selected by religions and

political characters. For instance, halal or legitimate food sources as well as the evasion of specific food varieties are markers of confidence. Hindus, Seventh Day Adventists,

Sikhs and Buddhists additionally have food customs that express conviction, character

also, social attachment.

John and Linda Stanley give, in this eloquent book, informed, experience-based bits of knowledge into the peculiarity of food the travel industry. They picked the

term 'food the travel industry' over 'culinary the travel industry' for this book since it is more

comprehensive and less 'elitist'. Absolutely the Stanleys are open to composing about upscale eating encounters, yet they are similarly at home coming by

a homestead entryway to get bread or eggs from a neighborhood rancher. Food the travel industry, as a

idea, covers the range from shopping at a neighborhood ranchers' market to eating

at a three-featured Michelin café.

Grounded in long stretches of involvement in food and culinary organizations, the creators will give you a rich comprehension of the intricate details of

food the travel industry, from its definition, through its clients, to the turn of events,

the board and promoting of a food the travel industry business. They finish up this

entrancing book with expectations about the fate of food the travel industry - once more, in light of their experience of working with food the travel industry administrators, retailers

also, makers.

The creators comprehend both the interest and supply sides (clients what's more, business) of food the travel industry as well as the numerous features of food the travel industry. All these shape the items in this educational book. Thus, this book has

something to offer not just the providers of food the travel industry items and encounters, however specialists and researchers also.

The book opens by considering the idea of food the travel industry from both the buyers' and the ranchers' points of view. The creators then look at the expected advantages of food the travel industry as well as its difficulties. They pose the inquiries anybody considering becoming engaged with food the travel industry ought to inquire:

would it be advisable for them they engage in food the travel industry or what the ramifications are of

welcoming people in general on to your homestead. For instance, there are numerous contemplations covering wellbeing and security of guests, creature wellbeing, obligation, the

requests of promoting and tasks of a food the travel industry business, and the

development of a business system and activity plans.

A focal worry for any travel industry business is understanding and serving an undeniably assorted and informed market - one that looks for 'nearby' and 'valid' flavors and encounters. The creators respond to this by portraying the contemporary food traveler and how she or he is evolving. These progressions incorporate segment and monetary movements as well as expansions in schooling, travel, and a developing interest for what some others have called 'insight'

as an element of the purported 'experience economy'. Tasting, getting ready and

finding out about food in its bunch structures is quintessentially an 'encounter' in

this post-current utilization of the term.

The Stanleys offer reasonable bits of knowledge

and guidance in view of their long stretches of

counseling. They will illuminate you about how food can be effectively showcased as a travel industry or diversion item. Whether your emphasis is on the

ranch or off the homestead activities, this book will furnish you with counsel about introducing, advancing and bundling food encounters and items. They

take the peruser on a stunning visit through heap signs of food

counting food production lines and historical centers, ranches and gardens, food and

facilities, food trucks and road markets. However, you will be directed a wide assortment of eating encounters from top notch food to air terminal cafés.

Also, they lead us through an educated conversation regarding food the travel industry showcasing.

Showcasing methodologies and stages cover a possibly baffling scope of

conceivable outcomes from side of the road signs to the Web. From showcasing strategies to the utilization of culinary the travel industry as an objective situating system, this book

investigates all.

Thus, hone your hunger and your interest. You are going to plunk down

to a feast of thoughts and data. Bon appétit!

Stephen Smith

School of Accommodation, Food, and The travel industry The executives

College of Guelph

Guelph, Ontario, Canada

Walk 2014

Foreword xv

Prelude

Food the travel industry is one of the quickest developing areas of the vacationer market

furthermore, covers numerous parts of the food and the travel industry. Composing a book tending to the necessities of that market is a test. There has never been a

book that has attempted to connect with the travel industry administrators all over the planet giving

the viable data they need to work on their business as well as trying

to zero in on the necessities of scholastics and understudies.

That is the point of this book. Try not to peruse this

anticipating a hypothetical book

that glances at research top to bottom; the point of this book is to address the requirements of

the useful the travel industry administrator and to give rules on how the business

can be created at a large scale and miniature level. In any case, in doing that, we

additionally trust that it will give rules and inspiration to understudies who are entering this developing and energizing industry.

Despite the fact that we truly do come from a scholastic foundation, a large portion of our work

is straightforwardly with the travel industry administrators assisting them with fostering their organizations.

We consequently accept this book can give a novel understanding into this market.

We have done whatever it takes not to be idealists. We want to check the wide range out

of travelers and their assumptions and to assist perusers with figuring out what they

are searching for in food the travel industry.

Food the travel industry used to zero in on ranch markets, cafés, food nurseries and ranchers' business sectors or shops. The assumption today is much more extensive

as driving retailers presently look on the food experience as a way to lock in

their clients. The travel industry administrators today understand that food the travel industry truth be told

covers numerous spectra. A portion of the areas examined in this book may not be considered as food the travel industry by certain perfectionists, however we accept they are regions

that should be examined as the edges of food the travel industry become more obscured

as time passes.

Retail and traveler innovation is changing quicker now than it has at any point finished also, perusers of this book should peruse further as innovation is progressing

so quickly. At the point when you get this book there will have been specialized advances

that have occurred between when it was composed and before you read it;

that is important for the tomfoolery and valuable open doors that we are looking in the business.

Our point is to animate discussion and assist the business with prospering, with

this book being one of the fundamental pieces of your tool stash to accomplish that objective.

John and Linda Stanley

John Stanley Partners

PO Box 200, Nannup, WA 6275 Australia

john@johnstanley.com.au

I Food The travel industry and the Vacationer

The world has become acclimated with the travel industry. As indicated by the World

The travel industry Organization1

a vacationer is 'going to and remaining in places outside their standard climate for not more than one sequential year for relaxation, business or different purposes.' In 2012 more than 1 billion of us were travelers and

as vacationers we spent over US$1.03 trillion. In 2012 China turned into the greatest

traveler spenders as a country, burning through US$102 billion on vacationer exercises.

As indicated by Funk and Wagnall,2

the distinction between a traveler and a

guest is that a guest is 'one who visits a region inside their neighborhood.'

'Food the travel industry' might be another arrangement of words on the vacationer scene. Indeed

however the principal manual for food the travel industry was written in 1931, Guida Gastronomica

d'Italia,

3

food the travel industry is as yet looked on as something new and in vogue.

Food the travel industry in many districts of the world has been and should be

coordinated into conventional the travel industry exercises, albeit in certain areas,

for instance in France and Italy, it is turning into the primary motivation to visit the objective.

The brilliant thing about this sort of the travel industry is that it is an every minute of every day, worldwide

also, accessible 365 days of the year action. The creators have been up at 3 am

in Japan to join a line of sightseers to visit the Tsukiji Market4

 in Tokyo (www.

tsukiji-market.or.jp) and endured the snow of Vermont in New Britain, in

the sugaring season in Spring to taste maple syrup (www.vermontmaple.

org). At Christmas the Christmas markets of Prague (Czech Republic) and

Germany are presently significant vacation spots with a worldwide market. Numerous finance managers may not consider they are in food the travel industry. Ask the

larger part of travelers visiting the UK interestingly the thing they are going to

do when they show up and one normal response is to visit an English bar. This

has turned into a genuine vacationer experience, yet the number of publicans that would order

themselves as working in the travel industry?

(J. Stanley and L. Stanley) 3

1 Presentation

What is Food The travel industry?

The travel industry is encountering quick development. As indicated by Jane Chang of Chang

Siblings Travel in Singapore, when she was evaluated in Walk 2014,5

the development in food the travel industry has been 30% every year for the last 10 years with

food visits to China, South Korea, Taiwan, Hong Kong, Australia, New

Zealand and Turkey being the most famous. In Singapore itself a one billion

Singapore dollar store was reported in 2012 to foster the travel industry, including

food the travel industry, and State leader Lee added piece of the mystery was 'High

Contact' and 'Super advanced' business improvement in the sector.6

A decade prior the Food The travel industry Affiliation was shaped, which now

goes under the name of the World Food Travel Affiliation (WFTA; www.

worldfoodtravel.org). The WFTA is situated in Portland, Oregon and its point

is to universally create and advance food the travel industry. Their definition

of food the travel industry is where we ought to begin our excursion: ' The pursuit and

satisfaction in extraordinary and significant food and drink encounters, both far

also, close.'

Food the travel industry has been picking up speed over the course of the past ten years around

the world for two fundamental reasons. Initial, a longing for individuals to find

where their food comes from and second to find new food sources and food

arrangements.

The test is where does food the travel industry start and finish. The number of of the current exercises did on the homestead are the travel industry exercises in the

perspective on the voyager? A visit to a ranchers' market is many times refered to as a traveler

movement, though a visit to the general store previously, to buy something similar

item, was not delegated a traveler movement. Having said that we now have the 'Waitrose Impact'. This is where a particular food retailer, for example,

Waitrose in the UK, has such a profoundly beneficial brand notoriety that house

costs around the store increment as it is a particularly helpful spot to shop. This

impact was accounted for by the BBC News in the UK.7

Research by Savills, the

bequest specialists (www.savills.co.uk), demonstrates that house costs in regions where

there is a Waitrose store are regularly 25% higher than the UK normal. In

London, there is a half premium in Waitrose postcodes.

The Everyday Mail Online8

 paper in the UK announced:
' It's Christmas

merriment for Waitrose, however Sainsbury's endure - customers flood to upmarket chain to

purchase Heston embraced items.' The article proceeded to make sense of that television VIP culinary specialist Heston Blumenthal supported a scope of items coming up and deals

leading the pack up to Christmas 2013 expanded by 4.1% against a Sainsbury's development of 0.2%. This implied that 22,000 items a moment were sold by

Waitrose on 23 December 2013, featuring the impact big name gourmet experts

have on food retailing and food the travel industry in the UK.

In Austin, Texas, the Wholefoods store at The Space squeezes into our

meaning of food the travel industry. It has an open air brew and bratwurst bar, is a setting for unrecorded music, has a Texas Ramen bar (sushi-style individual dishes),

11 different seating regions, an indoor clam bar, a local gathering place

what's more, has nearby specialists' compositions and craftsmanship showed around the store.

It is progressively evident that the hole among the travel industry and retailing as we comprehended it is mixing and that food the travel industry could now incorporate the

week after week food shop.

Ranchers are likewise jumping into the new turns of events. In Chicago,

Illinois, situated close to Dunkin Doughnuts on North Clark Road, you will find

the Rancher's Cooler: a candy machine created by Luke Saunders selling sound natural food from the ranch

in recyclable containers
(www.farmersfridge.com).

These improvements are
completely based around
food drawing in guests to a

certain region. Whether they
ought to be remembered for
a book on food the travel
industry we

are certain will cause banter.
The creators' methodology
has been to set the net wide

Fig. 1.1. ' Never Shop while
starving' in Shower Spa, UK.

Presentation 5

to guarantee inclusion of as numerous perspectives that we can on the culinary traveler's

venture, and ideally move the peruser to consider fresh.

Customer Consciousness of Food The travel industry

During the 1970s the customer turned out to be more mindful of the various sorts of food accessible and the nature of food they were devouring. Preceding this most

shoppers depended on the nearby general store or supermarket, which thusly,

to get by, advanced into away food corridors. Simultaneously

however, another development began; the improvement of ranchers' business sectors furthermore, ranch retail encounters. This thusly was trailed by a flood in food

programs on television and the appearance of the big name culinary experts who today, in numerous

nations, are basically as well known as heroes.

In 1945 the Food and Farming Association of the Unified Countries

set up World Food Day9

on 16 October every year. The first point was

to assist with growing further interest in food beginnings and point out the

food predicament in underdeveloped nations. Every year the occasion has an alternate

topic and turns out to be more perceived as a significant date in the schedule.

Albeit initially centered around forestalling

starvation, throughout the long term the day

has created to have a more extensive allure and incorporates maintainability and the starting points of food.

An ever increasing number of customers are presently needing to know not just where

their food is coming from, they need to visit the source and experience new food varieties as they travel. Additionally they need to explore actually in better approaches for

increasing the value of food. Accordingly more independent ventures are reaching out

in food the travel industry. For instance, in France there are north of 246 assortments of cheddar

being created and in the UK north of 700 assortments of cheese.10

The Worldwide Cheddar Grants (www.globalcheeseawards.com) are held in

Somerset in the UK. In 2013 they decided in favor of a Canadian cheddar as the best

cheddar on the planet; this was a rich gouda style Lankaaster cheddar from

Ontario made by Margaret Peters.

In 2010 the Global Culinary The travel industry Affiliation united with the New Zealand-based Global Culinary The travel industry Advancement

to deliver the 'Condition of the Culinary The travel Industry Report'.11 This recognized the most pre-arranged districts of the world for culinary the travel industry. The top

three arranged by positioning were Scotland, Louisiana, and Ontario. The least ready, yet the one with the most potential, was South Africa. Peru had

its own Facebook page to foster the market in that country, the one to focus on

to have done as such (www.facebook.com/perumuchogusto).

Key Drivers of Culinary The travel industry - A Customer Point of view

According to a customer's point of view the drivers are

wide and fluctuated, yet can be

summed up as follows.

6 Section 1

Expanded mindfulness in better sustenance

Numerous customers are presently more wellbeing cognizant or need to be more wellbeing

cognizant and are accordingly ready to look for better food choices, whether this be at a food store or homestead.

Food abandons actually exist in numerous urban communities, yet this is additionally acquiring public

consideration and activity is beginning to occur to further develop wellbeing principles.

This effectively reminds more wealthy purchasers about the significance of

wellbeing food sources. As indicated by the Food

Strengthening Project,12 a food desert

can be depicted as 'A geographic region where occupants' admittance to reasonable,

quality food choices (particularly new products of the soil) is confined or

nonexistent because of the shortfall of supermarkets inside helpful voyaging

distance'. A report ready for the US Congress by the Monetary Exploration

Administration of the US Branch of Farming 13 assessed around 2.3 million

individuals in the USA live more than 1 pretty far from a general store and do

not approach quality food.

Food exposure with respect to food abandons has been advanced through metropolitan

ranchers, for example, Ron Finley in Los Angeles, California, Will Allen from the

US mid-west, who was casted a ballot one of the top Time Magazine 100 of every 2010, and

Robin Emmons, who is one of the CNN 2013 Heroes14 (these are granted

yearly by the CNN Television station in the USA).

An inexorably urbanized society

An ever increasing number of individuals are moving to urban communities and the urbanization of the world's populace is occurring quickly. A lot more prosperous metropolitan occupants are

Fig. 1.2. Apple assortments available to be purchased at a ranch shop.

Presentation 7

presently searching for encounters beyond the city and need to reconnect with

rustic networks and nearby food varieties.

Maturing populace

Numerous western social orders are maturing quickly. Maturing People born after WW2 in western

social orders for the most part have huge dispensable salaries and are ready to

pay something else for a quality food experience. They have outfitted their homes,

established their nurseries and presently hope to spend their money another way.

They are purchasing less per shopping endeavor, yet are going to food outlets

on a more regular basis and are in this manner liable to be presented to additional fascinating food sources.

This maturing populace is searching for what the vacationer business calls 'delicate'

the travel industry. Here there is an opportunity for growth like in food or then again culinary the travel industry. They need exercises that are protected, instructive and with

no actual gamble as in bungee hopping for instance.

Numerous Asian social orders don't have this maturing Person born after WW2 factor. All things considered

they have an enormous area of well-off more youthful working class purchasers who are presently becoming worldwide vacationers and are searching for new encounters; in the

future these will be significant worldwide culinary sightseers.

Feasting out has expanded in prominence

In Canada and the USA the greater part of the typical family food spending plan is

presently spent on feasting out. This implies that many

individuals are being presented to

new food varieties and better quality food varieties. Accordingly, eateries keep on opening

also, extend, in addition to eating out urges purchasers to be more trial

also, attempt more fascinating food sources.

Ranches as a pleasant family objective

Customers search for 'work day accommodation' and 'end of the week encounters' and

a ranch is an incredible spot to go for such an encounter. Many schools are currently empowering youngsters to visit ranches as a growth opportunity to fathom where their food comes from and have a good time insight in a whiz climate. This thusly makes 'irritate power', where youngsters empower

their folks to take them to the homestead and invest more energy in the open country.

The Web

The Web has turned into the significant wellspring of data and has now been

acknowledged by the more extensive local area as the principal scan apparatus for finding new data. Culinary travelers currently plan their schedule on the web and in the

solace of their own home.

8 Part 1

Key Drivers for Food The travel industry - A Rancher Viewpoint

Before we check out at improvement of food the travel industry according to a homestead viewpoint we ought to think about back the improvement of the homestead.

A short history of the ranch retail time

Pre-1900: the Ranch Time

This was a period when ranchers and producers developed crops. Customers basically

went to their own nearby market and gotten their produce. No one tested the cycle; it was the state of affairs done. Take a visit to country

Spain or Italy and this framework is still set up.

1900–1950: the Creation Arranged Time

During this period ranchers and producers began understanding that they would be able

both develop huge scope harvests and attempt and impact the inventory network to purchase what they developed. The deals time had begun to show up. The principal general store

was opened in 1916 in Memphis, Tennessee when Clarence Saunders opened

his Piggly Wiggly store.

1950–2000: the Market-Arranged Time

Stores developed during this period into a market prevailing position, being the 'highest point of brain' decision for staple things. Organizations began to do

research on shoppers and their necessities and needs fully intent on fulfilling

shoppers wants. New produce assortments began to be created and the

shopper was offered a more extensive decision of produce from around the world. This is the time when numerous purchasers lost how they might interpret occasional food varieties.

2000–2050: the Intuitive People group

We are presently toward the beginning of another time when correspondences will be the key

to progress. The retailer and rancher can never again direct to the buyer.

We presently have shoppers who feel engaged and who need to argue.

Clients are utilizing a variety of apparatuses to speak with producers and retailers

also, they anticipate that industry should stay aware of their way of life. Furthermore, they

have altered their perspective set and are currently checking out at food another way what's more, are ready to scan out new roads for getting food.

In numerous nations as of late ranches close to metropolitan regions, which are

undeniably arranged for food the travel industry, have been extracted from presence due

to metropolitan strain for building land. These homesteads are an important item to society. As indicated by research by Teacher Trevor Move at La Trobe

College in Australia, 25% of the dollar worth of food created for human

utilization in Australia is developed on the edges of cities.15 Ranches close to

urban communities not just have a chance to zero in on the vacationer potential, yet in addition

are required for the fundamental food creation.

Urban areas, like Barcelona in Spain and Milan in Italy, have created

'rural parks' to protect the farmland around their urban communities and to make

Presentation 9

the travel industry open doors. In 2015, between 1 May and 31 October, the General

Global Composition in Milan centers around 'Taking care of the Planet, Energy for

Life', and the agrarian park set up by Politecnico di Milano, Slow Food Italia

also, the Universita di Scienza Gastronomiche will be finished as a feature of

the work. The horticultural park incorporates a ranchers' market, nearby breadmaking, a helpful store, pick your own and '0 Miles The travel industry'.

Most ranchers and homestead associations all

over the planet have not reached

this degree of collaboration and are fostering their own systems. These

remember settling on choices for whether the future ought to spin around the

'long order of things' or the 'short order of things.'

Numerous ranchers throughout recent many years have depended on the 'long chain food network' to get their produce to the shopper. They have zeroed in on

raising or developing the 'crude' item and transportation it through the circulation

network channels to a probable customer will be somewhere far off

or on the other hand even abroad.

The 'long pecking order' is as yet fundamental for the

progress of the world; agreeing

to the Unified Countries there are 193 nations on the planet, with 26 of these

nations creating 82% of the world's harvests. The 'long pecking order' is as yet a

genuinely necessary stockpile framework.

The 'long pecking order network' has worked for a long time. For instance in the USA in 1980 the normal rancher got 35 pennies of the retail food dollar.

Yet, throughout the long term, the production network has gradually pressed ranchers and in 2013 the typical American rancher was getting 8 pennies of the retail food dollar for

a similar ware.

Food miles

The other component that has become possibly the

most important factor is 'food miles'.

The meaning of a food mile is 'a mile over which a food thing is moved

during the excursion from maker to customer, as a unit of estimation of the

fuel used to move it.' Unnecessary food miles are the quickest developing source

of ozone harming substance discharges around the world. Food is being moved across nations and landmasses in long stretch vehicles that frequently need a cooler to keep

produce fresher. Also produce is transported from the northern side of the equator to the

southern half of the globe as well as the other way around by means of long stretch air flights.

The typical American potato in 2013 went north of 2000 miles from producer to buyer and the typical tomato 1569 miles.16 This isn't simply

occurring in the USA, the typical Swedish breakfast ventures 24,901 miles17

also, the main 29 food things in an Australian grocery store shopping basket travel

43,994 miles or 70,803 km.18

To make matters more confounded ranches, travelers and customers need to consider the benefit of decreasing 'food miles' alongside its 'carbon impression'.

A carbon impression is characterized as 'how much carbon dioxide delivered into

the environment because of the exercises of a specific individual, association, or local area'. It very well might be more supportable not to develop or deliver some food locally yet to import it from one more piece of the nation or from

abroad. For instance, is it more reasonable to deliver tomatoes with a low

'food mile' in a glasshouse in the UK or to import field-developed

tomatoes with a low carbon impression from a Mediterranean country?

These are issues that makers should examine with culinary vacationers when they visit a homestead. Numerous food sightseers are befuddled by the upsides of

food miles versus carbon impressions.

The 'short pecking order network' turned into another option and this is where

food the travel industry has an extraordinary fascination with the rancher. A more limited network where the rancher has more command over the produce, keeps a greater amount of the retail food dollar

also, draws in with the customer presently requests to numerous ranchers and cultivators.

One of the worldwide forerunners in 'short pecking order' believing is Joel Salatin of Polyface Homestead from Swoope in the Shenandoah Valley, Virginia (www.

polyfacefarms.com). He and his family accept that what's in store is about harmonious connections on the ranch and including the local area and visitors.19

His homestead thinking can be seen on http://vimeo.com/81468461.

The travel industry is one of the fundamental drivers of the economies of numerous nations

all over the planet. As the business has developed it

has sectioned into various classifications. A few areas of the travel industry have expanded in ubiquity though

different regions have found it more testing to develop their market section.

Food The travel industry Advancement

Food the travel industry is one the three key vacationer drivers all over the planet and as a result is acquiring media openness. It is hard to pinpoint when food

the travel industry created.

Numerous specialists accept the standard interest truly began with wine

the travel industry and has developed into food in the entirety of its angles. The wine makers of

Australia, Canada, France, South Africa and the USA were viewed as the pioneers of wine the travel industry. They saw the potential and differentiated from just

being grape plantations into connecting their office to eateries and general provincial

amusement.

Because of this cultivators and makers in the food creation industry saw the chance for broadening and went into the culinary

the travel industry area.

In the UK and the USA ranchers have generally been more proactive

in food retailing than in numerous different nations. Associations, for example, the

Public Homestead Retail and Promoting Affiliation (FARMA) in the UK and

The North American Homestead Direct Promoting Affiliation (NAFMA) in the

USA are both 'top' bodies for the retail area of cultivating that have been

laid out for a long time.

Shoppers are likewise now more worried about food security and need

to know where their food is coming from. The 2012/13 UK alarm on horse

meat being sold as hamburger meat assisted with making more shoppers more mindful of food security.

Closely involved individuals and associations are currently uniting to assist with advancing culinary the travel industry. For instance in 2010 Ed Walker, the Gourmet specialist Teacher

Presentation 11

at Thompson Waterways College, Kamloops, English Columbia, Canada was

enlivened to shape Farm2Chefs

(www.farm2chefs.com), which depends on

Island Gourmet specialists Cooperative in Victoria, English Columbia. This not-for-benefit

association has a mission to interface neighborhood ranchers with nearby eateries

to assist with supporting nearby ranchers and food security. Farm2Chefs presently has over

70 ranchers and cooks cooperating to advance nearby food and create

the travel industry in the locale.

Food information is currently essential for the school educational plan at numerous lesser

schools all over the planet and this is likewise assisting another age with becoming

more food mindful.

The other two significant vacationer development classes that are normal to numerous

nations are clinical and provincial the travel industry.

Clinical the travel industry

Sightseers from numerous western nations are presently voyaging abroad for clinical medicines and fixes and this will increment as the populace increments what's more, ages. This action won't be examined in this book, however perusers need

to know about this development as it very well might be an open door in the a few districts

of the existence where home grown plants could be essential for the cure programs.

The creators have seen the development of clinical the travel industry in Hungary and the amazing open doors it gives to rustic economies.

Provincial the travel industry

In the past it was the situation that vacationers were at first drawn to explicit symbol vacationer areas, like Paris, London or New York. The present vacationer

is much more bold and needs to search out provincial and wild places; this

has brought about an expansion in ecotourism.

Ecotourism covers various exercises. That's what the primary goal is

the guest leaves the region in the equivalent or a preferred condition over when they

shown up. Frequently they will become associated with protecting or improving the

climate they are visiting (see box).

Is it 'slow food' or 'food the travel industry'?

In 1986 Carlo Petrini, an Italian, began Slow Food Global (www.slowfood.com). He began the development on the grounds that Mcdonald's, the American

cheap food retailer, needed to have a store at the Spanish Strides in Rome and it

was obvious that cheap food outlets were beginning to enter the urban communities and making 'food deserts' and, thus, stoutness and diabetes was on the increment.

Carlo's point was to create attention to the financial stability of conventional food that was

in danger to stop the cycle as it was likewise obliterating the feel of

key vacationer areas.

12 Part 1

Box 1 Ecotourism - what's going on here?

It is helpful to put food the travel industry into the more extensive setting of contemporary thoughts regarding

the travel industry improvement, and particularly the idea of 'supportable the travel industry'. Manageable

the travel industry became well known in the mid 1990s as an off-shoot of 'manageable turn of events', a thought itself promoted in the last part of the 1980s as advancement that addresses the issues of present ages without compromising the capacity of people in the future to meet their own

needs.20 All the more functionally, and perceiving that there is no such thing as totally costfree the travel industry, practical the travel industry can be viewed as expected and made due so as to limit and augment the related expenses and advantages, separately,

both locally and globally.21 These expenses and advantages are ecological and sociocultural as

well as monetary, prompting far reaching support for 'triple primary concern' manageability that

considers every one of the three aspects at the equivalent time.22

Food the travel industry, with its attention on scrumptious and unmistakable food and drink, has clear allure for sightseers, but at the same time is progressively viewed as appealing by objective partners keen on turning out to be more manageable. The primary relationship with the monetary mainstay of the

triple main concern is that numerous culinary travelers are high-spending and knowledgeable purchasers who like to invest energy in an inclined toward objective, are bound to return, and are

ready to commend it to loved ones face to face and on friendly media.23

A more unpretentious association is that this burning through will in general firmly benefit the neighborhood economy,

since culinary travelers are chiefly keen on encountering

items and administrations that are

interesting to a specific objective. 100 bucks spent at a nearby occasion, for example, the

Manjimup Truffle Celebration in Western Australia, accordingly, is bound to go straightforwardly into the

pockets of neighborhood ranchers, producing in the process solid income 'multiplier impacts' inside the neighborhood and territorial economy.24

Positive ecological effects emerge from a similar craving to consume exceptional neighborhood

items. In a time where purchasers are bombarded with media inclusion of 'pink sludge', hereditarily adjusted groceries and widespread utilization of pesticides and antibiotics,25 there is (at any rate among the people who can manage the cost of it) an extraordinary longing to eat healthy and good food sources in the

where they are delivered. The distance of Tasmania was for quite some time viewed as a

the travel industry responsibility, yet this equivalent confinement is presently being advanced as a resource that conveys an picture of pure, new and delectable food.26 New Zealand has long perceived this

association in its stunningly fruitful '100 percent Unadulterated' promoting effort. As such a 'clean and

green' picture turns out to be more significant for drawing in vacationers, legislatures and different partners have a tremendous motivator to guarantee that the picture is exact, which benefits neighborhood inhabitants too. Locally, this may be reflected in the foundation of natural homesteads,

grass-took care of dairy cattle activities and supportable fish cafés. According to a worldwide viewpoint,

food the travel industry likewise assists in its own particular manner with decreasing the impacts of an Earth-wide temperature boost, creating a exceptionally low stock side 'carbon impression' due to neighborhood obtaining.

Higher neighborhood earnings and occupations from food the travel industry contribute fundamentally in their own

right to a more excellent of life among inhabitants, however strong sociocultural advantages too

bring about the way that this area advances objective

personality. ' Feeling of spot' is a term utilized

by geographers to depict the special blend of alluring qualities that separate a specific objective from any remaining objections, in this manner making it remarkably competitive.27 It is exceptionally simple to refer to Australian models - Lord Island cheddar, Barossa Valley wines,

Buderim ginger - and to take note of how every now and

again the nearby feeling of spot is both created

furthermore, reflected in different food celebrations. Such occasions produce and show major areas of strength for an of

local area pride, and can be truly significant for building social capital, that is to say, associations

furthermore, trust inside the community.28 These impacts are bound to little rustic networks, yet additionally figure increasingly more noticeably in the advertising of significant metropolitan

Proceeded

Presentation 13

The meaning of slow food on their site states:

Slow food remains at the junction of environment and gastronomy, morals and

joy. It goes against the normalization of taste and culture, and the over the top force of the food business multinationals and modern

farming. We accept everybody has a crucial right to the delight of

great food and thus the obligation to safeguard the legacy of food

custom and culture that makes this delight conceivable.

Carlo could be thought of as one of the initial architects of the culinary the travel industry development. In 1989 the development he began went global

with a statement in Paris and in 1990 they distributed the main registry,

'Osterie d'Italia'; a significant push ahead came in 1996 when the Salone del

Energy was laid out as a biennial occasion in Turin with the 'Ark of Taste'.

This occasion is presently a significant occasion and food

the travel industry fascination in the sluggish

food development where exhibitors from around the world presently take care of

advance their neighborhood food varieties.